VIOLIN

# 101 MOVIE HITS

Available for
FLUTE, CLARINET, ALTO SAX, TENOR SAX, TRUMPET,
HORN, TROMBONE, VIOLIN, VIOLA, CELLO

AF854560

ISBN 978-1-4950-6070-0

HAL•LEONARD®
CORPORATION
7777 W. Bluemound Rd. P.O. Box 13819 Milwaukee, WI 53213

For all works contained herein:
Unauthorized copying, arranging, adapting, recording, Internet posting, public performance,
or other distribution of the printed music in this publication is an infringement of copyright.
Infringers are liable under the law.

Visit Hal Leonard Online at
**www.halleonard.com**

# CONTENTS

# AGAINST ALL ODDS

(Take a Look at Me Now)

from AGAINST ALL ODDS

VIOLIN

Words and Music by
PHIL COLLINS

© 1984 IMAGEM MUSIC, PHILIP COLLINS LTD. and EMI GOLDEN TORCH MUSIC CORP.
Exclusive Print Rights for EMI GOLDEN TORCH MUSIC CORP. Administered by ALFRED MUSIC
All Rights Reserved Used by Permission

# ALFIE

Theme from the Paramount Picture ALFIE

VIOLIN

Words by HAL DAVID
Music by BURT BACHARACH

**Slowly, freely**

Copyright © 1966 Sony/ATV Music Publishing LLC
Copyright Renewed
All Rights Administered by Sony/ATV Music Publishing LLC, 424 Church Street, Suite 1200, Nashville, TN 37219
International Copyright Secured All Rights Reserved

# AXEL F

Theme from the Paramount Motion Picture BEVERLY HILLS COP

VIOLIN

By HAROLD FALTERMEYER

Copyright © 1984, 1985 Sony/ATV Music Publishing LLC
All Rights Administered by Sony/ATV Music Publishing LLC, 424 Church Street, Suite 1200, Nashville, TN 37219
International Copyright Secured All Rights Reserved

# BABY ELEPHANT WALK

from the Paramount Picture HATARI!

VIOLIN

By HENRY MANCINI

Copyright © 1962 Sony/ATV Music Publishing LLC
Copyright Renewed
All Rights Administered by Sony/ATV Music Publishing LLC, 424 Church Street, Suite 1200, Nashville, TN 37219
International Copyright Secured All Rights Reserved

# BEAUTY AND THE BEAST

from Walt Disney's BEAUTY AND THE BEAST

VIOLIN

Music by ALAN MENKEN
Lyrics by HOWARD ASHMAN

**Moderately slow**

© 1991 Walt Disney Music Company and Wonderland Music Company, Inc.
All Rights Reserved. Used by Permission.

# BLAZE OF GLORY

featured in the film YOUNG GUNS II

VIOLIN

Words and Music by
JON BON JOVI

Copyright © 1990, 1992 Bon Jovi Publishing
All Rights Administered by Kobalt Songs Music Publishing
All Rights Reserved Used by Permission

# BLUE VELVET

featured in the Motion Picture BLUE VELVET

VIOLIN

Words and Music by BERNIE WAYNE and LEE MORRIS

Copyright © 1951 (Renewed 1979) Bernie Wayne Music and JLZ Music
All Rights for Bernie Wayne Music Controlled and Administered by Spirit One Music
All Rights for JLZ Music Administered by Lichelle Music Company
International Copyright Secured All Rights Reserved

# BORN FREE

from the Columbia Pictures' Release BORN FREE

VIOLIN

Words by DON BLACK
Music by JOHN BARRY

Copyright © 1966 Sony/ATV Music Publishing LLC
Copyright Renewed
All Rights Administered by Sony/ATV Music Publishing LLC, 424 Church Street, Suite 1200, Nashville, TN 37219
International Copyright Secured All Rights Reserved

# CALL ME

from the Paramount Motion Picture AMERICAN GIGOLO

VIOLIN

Words by DEBORAH HARRY
Music by GIORGIO MORODER

**Moderately fast**

Copyright © 1979, 1980 Sony/ATV Music Publishing LLC, BMG Monarch and Monster Island Music
All Rights on behalf of Sony/ATV Music Publishing LLC Administered by Sony/ATV Music Publishing LLC, 424 Church Street, Suite 1200, Nashville, TN 37219
All Rights on behalf of BMG Monarch and Monster Island Music Administered by BMG Rights Management (US) LLC
International Copyright Secured All Rights Reserved

2.

# CAN YOU FEEL THE LOVE TONIGHT

from Walt Disney Pictures' THE LION KING

VIOLIN

Music by ELTON JOHN
Lyrics by TIM RICE

© 1994 Wonderland Music Company, Inc.
All Rights Reserved. Used by Permission.

# CAN'T HELP FALLING IN LOVE

from the Paramount Picture BLUE HAWAII

VIOLIN

Words and Music by GEORGE DAVID WEISS,
HUGO PERETTI and LUIGI CREATORE

Copyright © 1961; Renewed 1989 Gladys Music (ASCAP)
All Rights in the U.S. Administered by Imagem Sounds
International Copyright Secured All Rights Reserved

# THE CANDY MAN

from WILLY WONKA AND THE CHOCOLATE FACTORY

VIOLIN

Words and Music by LESLIE BRICUSSE
and ANTHONY NEWLEY

Copyright © 1970, 1971 by Taradam Music, Inc.
Copyright Renewed
International Copyright Secured All Rights Reserved

# CHARIOTS OF FIRE

from CHARIOTS OF FIRE

VIOLIN

By VANGELIS

© 1981 EMI MUSIC PUBLISHING LTD.
All Rights in the United States and Canada Controlled and Administered by EMI APRIL MUSIC INC.
All Rights Reserved International Copyright Secured Used by Permission

# COLORS OF THE WIND

from Walt Disney's POCAHONTAS

VIOLIN

Music by ALAN MENKEN
Lyrics by STEPHEN SCHWARTZ

© 1995 Wonderland Music Company, Inc. and Walt Disney Music Company
All Rights Reserved. Used by Permission.

D.S. al Coda
CODA

# COME SATURDAY MORNING

(Saturday Morning)

from the Paramount Picture THE STERILE CUCKOO

VIOLIN

Words by DORY PREVIN
Music by FRED KARLIN

Copyright © 1969 Sony/ATV Music Publishing LLC
Copyright Renewed
All Rights Administered by Sony/ATV Music Publishing LLC, 424 Church Street, Suite 1200, Nashville, TN 37219
International Copyright Secured All Rights Reserved

# CUPS
## (When I'm Gone)
from the Motion Picture Soundtrack PITCH PERFECT

VIOLIN

Words and Music by A.P. CARTER,
LUISA GERSTEIN and HELOISE TUNSTALL-BEHRENS

Copyright © 2013 by Peer International Corporation and BMG Gold Songs
All Rights for BMG Gold Songs Administered by BMG Rights Management (US) LLC
International Copyright Secured All Rights Reserved
- contains a sample from "When I'm Gone" by A.P. Carter

# COME WHAT MAY

from the Motion Picture MOULIN ROUGE

VIOLIN

Words and Music by
DAVID BAERWALD

**Slowly**

Copyright © 2001 ALMO MUSIC CORP., ZEN OF INIQUITY and T C F MUSIC PUBLISHING, INC.
All Rights for ZEN OF INIQUITY Controlled and Administered by ALMO MUSIC CORP.
All Rights Reserved Used by Permission

# DANGER ZONE

from the Motion Picture TOP GUN

VIOLIN

Words and Music by GIORGIO MORODER
and TOM WHITLOCK

Copyright © 1986 Sony/ATV Music Publishing LLC and Budde Music, Inc.
All Rights on behalf of Sony/ATV Music Publishing LLC Administered by Sony/ATV Music Publishing LLC, 424 Church Street, Suite 1200, Nashville, TN 37219
All Rights on behalf of Budde Music, Inc. Administered by WB Music Corp.
International Copyright Secured All Rights Reserved

# DEAR HEART

from DEAR HEART

VIOLIN

Music by HENRY MANCINI
Words by JAY LIVINGSTON and RAY EVANS

Copyright © 1964 NORTHRIDGE MUSIC CO. and WITMARK-N-SONS
Copyright Renewed
All Rights Controlled and Administered by UNIVERSAL MUSIC CORP.
All Rights Reserved Used by Permission

# DIAMONDS ARE A GIRL'S BEST FRIEND

from GENTLEMEN PREFER BLONDES

VIOLIN

Words by LEO ROBIN
Music by JULE STYNE

Copyright © 1949 (Renewed) by Music Sales Corporation (ASCAP)
International Copyright Secured All Rights Reserved
Reprinted by Permission

# DO YOU KNOW WHERE YOU'RE GOING TO?

Theme from MAHOGANY

VIOLIN

Words by GERRY GOFFIN
Music by MICHAEL MASSER

Copyright © 1973 Screen Gems-EMI Music Inc. and Jobete Music Co., Inc.
Copyright Renewed
All Rights Administered by Sony/ATV Music Publishing LLC, 424 Church Street, Suite 1200, Nashville, TN 37219
International Copyright Secured All Rights Reserved

# DON'T YOU (FORGET ABOUT ME)

from the Universal Picture THE BREAKFAST CLUB

VIOLIN

Words and Music by KEITH FORSEY
and STEVE SCHIFF

Copyright © 1985 USI A MUSIC PUBLISHING and USI B MUSIC PUBLISHING
All Rights Controlled and Administered by UNIVERSAL MUSIC CORP. and SONGS OF UNIVERSAL, INC.
All Rights Reserved Used by Permission

# THE DREAME

from the film SENSE AND SENSIBILITY

VIOLIN

By PATRICK DOYLE

Copyright © 1995 ole New Colorful Picture Music
All Rights Administered by Sony/ATV Music Publishing LLC, 424 Church Street, Suite 1200, Nashville, TN 37219
International Copyright Secured All Rights Reserved

# END OF THE ROAD

from the Paramount Motion Picture BOOMERANG

VIOLIN

Words and Music by BABYFACE,
L.A. REID and DARYL SIMMONS

Copyright © 1992 Sony/ATV Music Publishing LLC, ECAF Music, Warner-Tamerlane Publishing Corp., Boobie-Loo Music and Green Skirt Music
All Rights on behalf of Sony/ATV Music Publishing LLC and ECAF Music Administered by
Sony/ATV Music Publishing LLC, 424 Church Street, Suite 1200, Nashville, TN 37219
All Rights on behalf of Boobie-Loo Music Administered by Warner-Tamerlane Publishing Corp.
International Copyright Secured All Rights Reserved

# ENDLESS LOVE

from ENDLESS LOVE

VIOLIN

Words and Music by
LIONEL RICHIE

Copyright © 1981 by PGP Music, Brockman Music and Brenda Richie Publishing
All Rights for PGP Music Administered by Intersong U.S.A., Inc.
International Copyright Secured All Rights Reserved

# EVERYBODY'S TALKIN'

(Echoes)

from MIDNIGHT COWBOY

VIOLIN

Words and Music by
FRED NEIL

Copyright © 1967 (Renewed) Third Palm Music (BMI)
Worldwide Rights owned by Arc Music, Inc. (Administered by BMG Rights Management (US) LLC)
All Rights Reserved Used by Permission

# EXHALE
## (Shoop Shoop)
from WAITING TO EXHALE

VIOLIN

Words and Music by
BABYFACE

Copyright © 1995 Sony/ATV Music Publishing LLC, ECAF Music and Fox Film Music Corporation
All Rights on behalf of Sony/ATV Music Publishing LLC and ECAF Music Administered by
Sony/ATV Music Publishing LLC, 424 Church Street, Suite 1200, Nashville, TN 37219
International Copyright Secured All Rights Reserved

# EYE OF THE TIGER

Theme from ROCKY III

VIOLIN

Words and Music by FRANK SULLIVAN
and JIM PETERIK

Copyright © 1982 Sony/ATV Music Publishing LLC, Rude Music, Three Wise Boys LLC, WB Music Corp. and Easy Action Music
All Rights on behalf of Sony/ATV Music Publishing LLC, Rude Music and Three Wise Boys LLC Administered by
Sony/ATV Music Publishing LLC, 424 Church Street, Suite 1200, Nashville, TN 37219
All Rights on behalf of Easy Action Music Administered by WB Music Corp.
International Copyright Secured All Rights Reserved

# FOOTLOOSE

Theme from the Paramount Motion Picture FOOTLOOSE

VIOLIN

Words by DEAN PITCHFORD
Music by KENNY LOGGINS

**Fast Rock**

Copyright © 1984 Sony/ATV Melody LLC and Sony/ATV Harmony LLC
All Rights by Sony/ATV Music Publishing LLC, 424 Church Street, Suite 1200, Nashville, TN 37219
International Copyright Secured All Rights Reserved

# FORREST GUMP – MAIN TITLE

(Feather Theme)

from the Paramount Motion Picture FORREST GUMP

VIOLIN

Music by ALAN SILVESTRI

Copyright © 1994 Sony/ATV Music Publishing LLC
All Rights Administered by Sony/ATV Music Publishing LLC, 424 Church Street, Suite 1200, Nashville, TN 37219
International Copyright Secured All Rights Reserved

# HALLELUJAH

featured in the DreamWorks Motion Picture SHREK

VIOLIN

Words and Music by
LEONARD COHEN

**Moderately slow, in 2**

Copyright © 1985 Sony/ATV Music Publishing LLC
All Rights Administered by Sony/ATV Music Publishing LLC, 424 Church Street, Suite 1200, Nashville, TN 37219
International Copyright Secured All Rights Reserved

# GLORY OF LOVE

Theme from KARATE KID PART II

VIOLIN

Words and Music by DAVID FOSTER,
PETER CETERA and DIANE NINI

Copyright © 1986 by Air Bear Music, Universal Music - MGB Songs, EMI Gold Horizon Music Corp. and EMI Golden Torch Music Corp.
All Rights for Air Bear Music Administered by Peermusic Ltd.
Exclusive Print Rights for EMI Gold Horizon Music Corp. and EMI Golden Torch Music Corp. Administered by Alfred Music
International Copyright Secured All Rights Reserved

# HAPPY

from DESPICABLE ME 2

VIOLIN

Words and Music by
PHARRELL WILLIAMS

Copyright © 2013 EMI April Music Inc., More Water From Nazareth and Universal Pictures Music
All Rights on behalf of EMI April Music Inc. and More Water From Nazareth Administered by
Sony/ATV Music Publishing LLC, 424 Church Street, Suite 1200, Nashville, TN 37219
All Rights on behalf of Universal Pictures Music Controlled and Administered by Universal Music Corp.
International Copyright Secured All Rights Reserved

# THE HEAT IS ON

from the Paramount Motion Picture BEVERLY HILLS COP

VIOLIN

Words by KEITH FORSEY
Music by HAROLD FALTERMEYER

**Moderately fast Rock**

Copyright © 1984, 1985 Sony/ATV Music Publishing LLC
All Rights Administered by Sony/ATV Music Publishing LLC, 424 Church Street, Suite 1200, Nashville, TN 37219
International Copyright Secured All Rights Reserved

# HELLO AGAIN

from the Motion Picture THE JAZZ SINGER

VIOLIN

Words by NEIL DIAMOND
Music by NEIL DIAMOND
and ALAN LINDGREN

© 1980, 1982 STONEBRIDGE MUSIC and SWEET SIXTEEN MUSIC, INC.
All Rights Reserved

# HOW DEEP IS YOUR LOVE

from the Motion Picture SATURDAY NIGHT FEVER

VIOLIN

Words and Music by BARRY GIBB,
ROBIN GIBB and MAURICE GIBB

Copyright © 1979 by Yvonne Gibb, The Estate Of Robin Gibb, Warner-Tamerlane Publishing Corp. and Crompton Songs LLC
All Rights for Yvonne Gibb and The Estate Of Robin Gibb Administered in the U.S. and Canada by Universal Music - Careers
All Rights for Crompton Songs LLC Administered by Warner-Tamerlane Publishing Corp.
International Copyright Secured All Rights Reserved

# I AM A MAN OF CONSTANT SORROW

featured in O BROTHER, WHERE ART THOU?

VIOLIN

Words and Music by
CARTER STANLEY

**Moderately, in 2**

Copyright © 1953 by Peer International Corporation
Copyright Renewed
International Copyright Secured All Rights Reserved

# I BELIEVE I CAN FLY

from SPACE JAM

VIOLIN

Words and Music by
ROBERT KELLY

Copyright © 1996 by Universal Music - Z Songs and R. Kelly Publishing
All Rights Administered by Universal Music - Z Songs
International Copyright Secured All Rights Reserved

# I JUST CALLED TO SAY I LOVE YOU

featured in THE WOMAN IN RED

VIOLIN

Words and Music by
STEVIE WONDER

**Moderately**

Copyright © 1984 Jobete Music Co., Inc. and Black Bull Music
All Rights Administered by Sony/ATV Music Publishing LLC, 424 Church Street, Suite 1200, Nashville, TN 37219
International Copyright Secured All Rights Reserved

# I WILL ALWAYS LOVE YOU

featured in THE BODYGUARD

VIOLIN

Words and Music by
DOLLY PARTON

Copyright © 1973 (Renewed 2001) Velvet Apple Music
All Rights Reserved Used by Permission

# I WILL WAIT FOR YOU

from THE UMBRELLAS OF CHERBOURG

VIOLIN

Music by MICHEL LEGRAND
Original French Text by JACQUES DEMY
English Words by NORMAN GIMBEL

Copyright © 1965 UNIVERSAL - SONGS OF POLYGRAM INTERNATIONAL, INC., JONWARE MUSIC CO.,
LES PRODUCTIONS FRANCIS LEMARQUE, LES PRODUCTIONS MICHEL LEGRAND and WORDS WEST LLC
English Words Renewed by NORMAN GIMBEL and Assigned to WORDS WEST LLC (P.O. Box 15187, Beverly Hills, CA 90209 USA)
All Rights Reserved Used by Permission

# (I'VE HAD) THE TIME OF MY LIFE

from DIRTY DANCING

VIOLIN

Words and Music by FRANKE PREVITE,
JOHN DeNICOLA and DONALD MARKOWITZ

Copyright © 1987 Knockout Music, RU Cyrius Publishing, Calspen Music, Sony/ATV Music Publishing LLC, Damusic Co., Inc. and Marcu Music Company, Inc.
All Rights on behalf of Sony/ATV Music Publishing LLC Administered by Sony/ATV Music Publishing LLC, 424 Church Street, Suite 1200, Nashville, TN 37219
International Copyright Secured All Rights Reserved

# JAILHOUSE ROCK

from JAILHOUSE ROCK

VIOLIN

Words and Music by JERRY LEIBER
and MIKE STOLLER

**Moderately**

Copyright © 1957 Sony/ATV Music Publishing LLC
Copyright Renewed
All Rights Administered by Sony/ATV Music Publishing LLC, 424 Church Street, Suite 1200, Nashville, TN 37219
International Copyright Secured All Rights Reserved

# THE JOHN DUNBAR THEME

from DANCES WITH WOLVES

VIOLIN

By JOHN BARRY

© 1990 EMI BLACKWOOD MUSIC INC., AFFIRMED MUSIC and DONNA DIJON MUSIC PUBLICATIONS
All Rights for AFFIRMED MUSIC Controlled and Administered by EMI BLACKWOOD MUSIC INC.
All Rights for DONNA DIJON MUSIC PUBLICATIONS Administered by SONY/ATV MUSIC PUBLISHING LLC, 424 Church Street, Suite 1200, Nashville, TN 37219
All Rights Reserved International Copyright Secured Used by Permission

# KOKOMO

from the Motion Picture COCKTAIL

VIOLIN

Words and Music by JOHN PHILLIPS,
TERRY MELCHER, MIKE LOVE,
and SCOTT McKENZIE

© 1988 Touchstone Pictures Music & Songs, Inc., Spirit Two Music, Inc., Buena Vista Music Company,
Daywin Music, Inc., Clairaudient Music Corporation and Spirit One Music
All Rights Reserved Used by Permission

# LET THE RIVER RUN

Theme from the Motion Picture WORKING GIRL

VIOLIN

Words and Music by
CARLY SIMON

Copyright © 1989 C'est Music and T C F Music Publishing, Inc.
All Rights for C'est Music Administered by BMG Rights Management (US) LLC
All Rights Reserved Used by Permission

# LET IT GO

from Disney's Animated Feature FROZEN

VIOLIN

Music and Lyrics by KRISTEN ANDERSON-LOPEZ
and ROBERT LOPEZ

© 2013 Wonderland Music Company, Inc.
All Rights Reserved. Used by Permission.

Fine
D.S. al Fine

# LIVE AND LET DIE

from LIVE AND LET DIE

VIOLIN

Words and Music by PAUL McCARTNEY
and LINDA McCARTNEY

© 1973 (Renewed) PAUL and LINDA McCARTNEY and UNITED ARTISTS MUSIC LTD.
All Rights for UNITED ARTISTS MUSIC LTD. Assigned to and Controlled by EMI UNART CATALOG INC.
Exclusive Print Rights for EMI UNART CATALOG INC. Controlled and Administered by ALFRED MUSIC
All Rights Reserved Used by Permission

# THE LOOK OF LOVE

from CASINO ROYALE

VIOLIN

Words by HAL DAVID
Music by BURT BACHARACH

© 1967 (Renewed 1995) COLGEMS-EMI MUSIC INC.
All Rights Reserved International Copyright Secured Used by Permission

# LUCK BE A LADY

from GUYS AND DOLLS

VIOLIN

By FRANK LOESSER

© 1950 (Renewed) FRANK MUSIC CORP.
All Rights Reserved

# A MAN AND A WOMAN

## (Un homme et une femme)

from A MAN AND A WOMAN

VIOLIN

Original Words by PIERRE BAROUH
English Words by JERRY KELLER
Music by FRANCIS LAI

Copyright © 1966 EDITIONS SARAVAH, Paris, France
Copyright Renewed
All Rights in the U.S. and Canada Controlled and Administered by UNIVERSAL MUSIC CORP.
All Rights Reserved Used by Permission

# MANIAC

from the Paramount Picture FLASHDANCE

VIOLIN

Words and Music by MICHAEL SEMBELLO
and DENNIS MATKOSKY

Copyright © 1983 Sony/ATV Music Publishing LLC, Intersong U.S.A., Inc. and WB Music Corp.
All Rights for Sony/ATV Music Publishing LLC Administered by Sony/ATV Music Publishing LLC, 424 Church Street, Suite 1200, Nashville, TN 37219
International Copyright Secured All Rights Reserved

# MISSION: IMPOSSIBLE THEME

from the Paramount Motion Picture MISSION: IMPOSSIBLE

VIOLIN

By LALO SCHIFRIN

Copyright © 1965 Sony/ATV Music Publishing LLC
Copyright Renewed
All Rights Administered by Sony/ATV Music Publishing LLC, 424 Church Street, Suite 1200, Nashville, TN 37219
International Copyright Secured All Rights Reserved

# MRS. ROBINSON

from THE GRADUATE

VIOLIN

Words and Music by
PAUL SIMON

Copyright © 1968, 1970 (Copyrights Renewed) Paul Simon (BMI)
International Copyright Secured All Rights Reserved
Reprinted by Permission of Music Sales Corporation

# MOON RIVER

from the Paramount Picture BREAKFAST AT TIFFANY'S

VIOLIN

Words by JOHNNY MERCER
Music by HENRY MANCINI

Copyright © 1961 Sony/ATV Music Publishing LLC
Copyright Renewed
All Rights Administered by Sony/ATV Music Publishing LLC, 424 Church Street, Suite 1200, Nashville, TN 37219
International Copyright Secured All Rights Reserved

# MORE

## (Ti guarderò nel cuore)

from the film MONDO CANE

VIOLIN

Music by NINO OLIVIERO and RIZ ORTOLANI
Italian Lyrics by MARCELLO CIORCIOLINI
English Lyrics by NORMAN NEWELL

Copyright © 1962 Creazioni Artistiche Musicali C.A.M. S.r.l. and Creative Team Inc.
Copyright Renewed
All Rights for Creazioni Artistiche Musicali C.A.M. S.r.l. in the U.S. and Canada Controlled and Administered by Sugar Song Publications Inc.
International Copyright Secured All Rights Reserved

# THE MUSIC OF GOODBYE

from OUT OF AFRICA

VIOLIN

Words and Music by JOHN BARRY,
ALAN BERGMAN and MARILYN BERGMAN

Copyright © 1986 UNIVERSAL MUSIC CORP. and SONGS OF UNIVERSAL, INC.
All Rights Reserved Used by Permission

# MY HEART WILL GO ON

## (Love Theme from 'Titanic')

from the Paramount and Twentieth Century Fox Motion Picture TITANIC

VIOLIN

Music by JAMES HORNER
Lyric by WILL JENNINGS

Copyright © 1997 Sony/ATV Harmony, Sony/ATV Melody, T C F Music Publishing, Inc., Fox Film Music Corporation and Blue Sky Rider Songs
All Rights on behalf of Sony/ATV Harmony and Sony/ATV Melody Administered by Sony/ATV Music Publishing LLC, 424 Church Street, Suite 1200, Nashville, TN 37219
All Rights on behalf of Blue Sky Rider Songs Administered by Irving Music, Inc.
International Copyright Secured All Rights Reserved

# NINE TO FIVE

from NINE TO FIVE

VIOLIN

Words and Music by
DOLLY PARTON

Copyright © 1980 Velvet Apple Music
All Rights Reserved Used by Permission

# NOTHING'S GONNA STOP US NOW

featured in MANNEQUIN

VIOLIN

Words and Music by DIANE WARREN
and ALBERT HAMMOND

**Moderate Rock**

Copyright © 1986, 1987 by Edition Sunset Publishing, Inc., Realsongs and Albert Hammond Music
All Rights for Edition Sunset Publishing, Inc. Administered by Universal Music - MGB Songs
All Rights for Albert Hammond Music Administered for the World
excluding the UK, Eire, Spain, Portugal, Mexico, Caribbean, Central and South America by Kobalt Songs Music Publishing
International Copyright Secured All Rights Reserved

1.
2.

# OLD TIME ROCK & ROLL

featured in RISKY BUSINESS

VIOLIN

Words and Music by GEORGE JACKSON
and THOMAS E. JONES III

**Medium Rock**

Copyright © 1977 by Peermusic III, Ltd. and Muscle Shoals Sound Publishing
Copyright Renewed
All Rights Administered by Peermusic III, Ltd.
International Copyright Secured All Rights Reserved

# THE PINK PANTHER

from THE PINK PANTHER

VIOLIN

By HENRY MANCINI

**Moderately, in 4**

Copyright © 1963 Northridge Music Company and EMI U Catalog Inc.
Copyright Renewed
All Rights on behalf of Northridge Music Company Administered by Spirit Two Music
Exclusive Print Rights for EMI U Catalog Inc. Controlled and Administered by Alfred Music
All Rights Reserved Used by Permission

# PUT YOUR DREAMS AWAY (FOR ANOTHER DAY)

featured in INSIDE MOVES

VIOLIN

Words by RUTH LOWE
Music by STEPHAN WEISS
and PAUL MANN

Copyright © 1942, 1943 by Chappell & Co. and BMG Firefly
Copyright Renewed
All Rights for BMG Firefly Administered by BMG Rights Management (US) LLC
All Rights Reserved Used by Permission

# PUTTIN' ON THE RITZ

from the Motion Picture PUTTIN' ON THE RITZ

VIOLIN

Words and Music by
IRVING BERLIN

**Moderately, in 2**

© Copyright 1928, 1929 by Irving Berlin
© Arrangement Copyright 1946 by Irving Berlin
Copyright Renewed
International Copyright Secured All Rights Reserved

# QUE SERA, SERA
## (Whatever Will Be, Will Be)

from THE MAN WHO KNEW TOO MUCH

VIOLIN

Words and Music by JAY LIVINGSTON
and RAYMOND B. EVANS

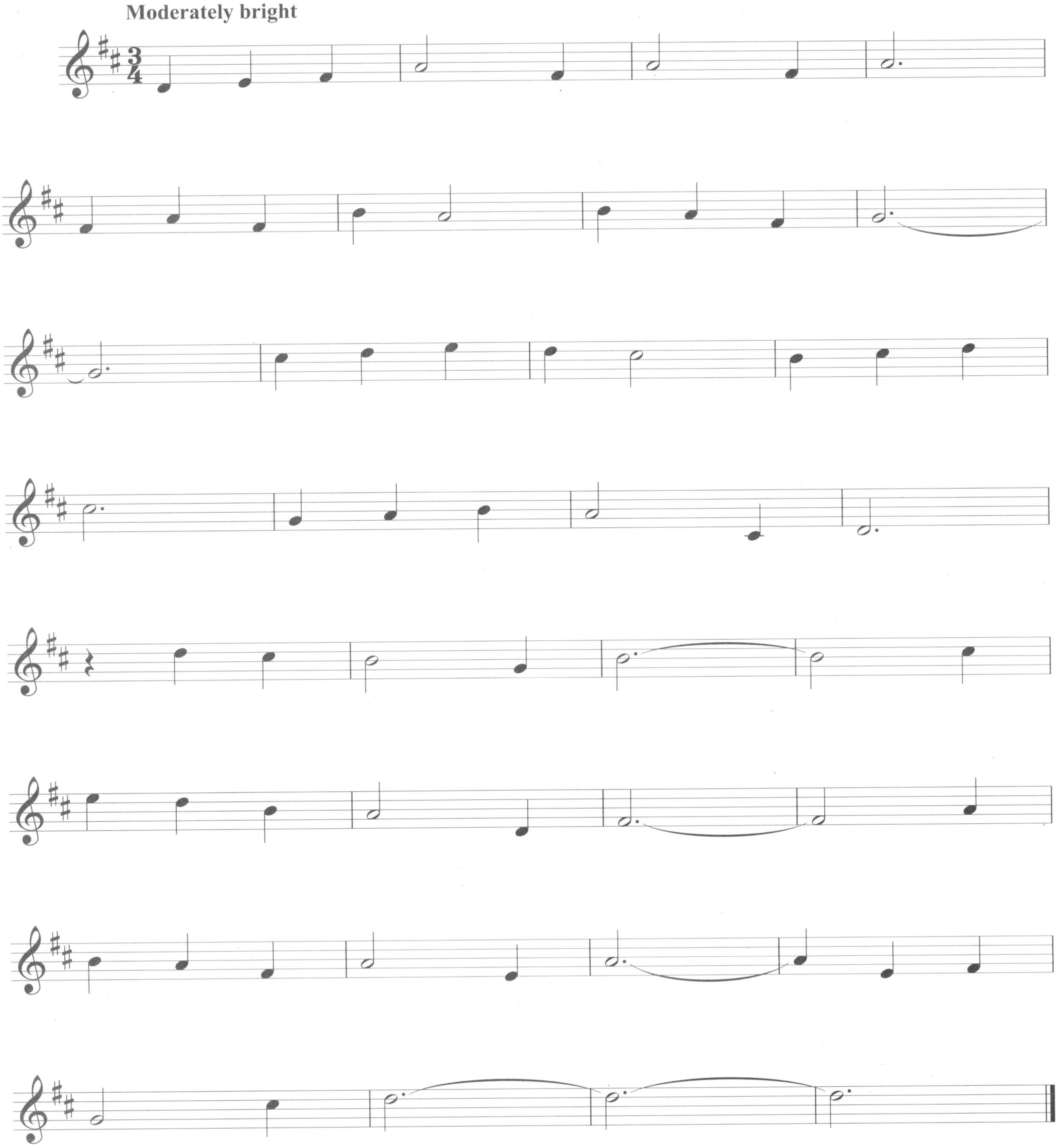


Copyright © 1955 by JAY LIVINGSTON MUSIC and ST. ANGELO MUSIC
Copyright Renewed
All Rights Reserved Used by Permission

# THE RAINBOW CONNECTION

from THE MUPPET MOVIE

VIOLIN

Words and Music by PAUL WILLIAMS
and KENNETH L. ASCHER

© 1979 Fuzzy Muppet Songs
All Rights Reserved. Used by Permission.

# RAINDROPS KEEP FALLIN' ON MY HEAD

from BUTCH CASSIDY AND THE SUNDANCE KID

VIOLIN

Lyrics by HAL DAVID
Music by BURT BACHARACH

Copyright © 1969 BMG Rights Management (UK) Ltd., New Hidden Valley Music Co. and WB Music Corp.
Copyright Renewed
All Rights Administered by BMG Rights Management (US) LLC
All Rights Reserved Used by Permission

# ROCK AROUND THE CLOCK

featured in the Motion Picture BLACKBOARD JUNGLE

VIOLIN

Words and Music by MAX C. FREEDMAN
and JIMMY DeKNIGHT

Copyright © 1953 Myers Music Inc., Kassner Associated Publishers Ltd. and Capano Music
Copyright Renewed
All Rights on behalf of Myers Music Inc. and Kassner Associated Publishers Ltd. Administered by
Sony/ATV Music Publishing LLC, 424 Church Street, Suite 1200, Nashville, TN 37219
International Copyright Secured All Rights Reserved

# LOVE THEME FROM "ST. ELMO'S FIRE"

from the Motion Picture ST. ELMO'S FIRE

VIOLIN

Words and Music by
DAVID FOSTER

Copyright © 1985 by Air Bear Music and EMI Gold Horizon Music Corp.
All Rights for Air Bear Music Administered by Peermusic Ltd.
International Copyright Secured All Rights Reserved

# SAY YOU, SAY ME

from the Motion Picture WHITE NIGHTS

VIOLIN

Words and Music by
LIONEL RICHIE

Copyright © 1985 by Brockman Music and Brenda Richie Publishing
All Rights Reserved Used by Permission

# SEPARATE LIVES

Love Theme from WHITE NIGHTS

VIOLIN

Words and Music by
STEPHEN BISHOP

Copyright © 1985 STEPHEN BISHOP MUSIC PUBLISHING, HIT & RUN MUSIC (PUBLISHING) LTD. and EMI GOLD HORIZON MUSIC CORP.
All Rights for STEPHEN BISHOP MUSIC PUBLISHING Controlled and Administered by UNIVERSAL MUSIC CORP.
All Rights for HIT & RUN MUSIC (PUBLISHING) LTD. Controlled and Administered by EMI BLACKWOOD MUSIC INC.
All Rights Reserved Used by Permission

Freely

# THE SHADOW OF YOUR SMILE

Love Theme from THE SANDPIPER

VIOLIN

Music by JOHNNY MANDEL
Words by PAUL FRANCIS WEBSTER

© 1965 METRO-GOLDWYN-MAYER, INC.
Copyright Renewed by EMI MILLER CATALOG INC. and MARISSA MUSIC
All Rights for EMI MILLER CATALOG INC. Controlled and Administered by EMI MILLER CATALOG INC. (Publishing) and ALFRED MUSIC (Print)
All Rights for MARISSA MUSIC Controlled and Administered by ALMO MUSIC CORP.
All Rights Reserved Used by Permission

# SOMEWHERE IN TIME

from SOMEWHERE IN TIME

VIOLIN

By JOHN BARRY

Copyright © 1980 USI B GLOBAL MUSIC PUBLISHING
All Rights Controlled and Administered by SONGS OF UNIVERSAL, INC.
All Rights Reserved Used by Permission

# SKYFALL

from the Motion Picture SKYFALL

VIOLIN

Words and Music by ADELE ADKINS
and PAUL EPWORTH

Copyright © 2012 MELTED STONE PUBLISHING LTD. and EMI MUSIC PUBLISHING LTD.
All Rights for MELTED STONE PUBLISHING LTD. in the U.S. and Canada Controlled and Administered by
UNIVERSAL - SONGS OF POLYGRAM INTERNATIONAL, INC.
All Rights for EMI MUSIC PUBLISHING LTD. Administered by SONY/ATV MUSIC PUBLISHING LLC, 424 Church Street, Suite 1200, Nashville, TN 37219
All Rights Reserved Used by Permission

D.S. al Coda
CODA

# SOMEWHERE, MY LOVE

Lara's Theme from DOCTOR ZHIVAGO

VIOLIN

Lyric by PAUL FRANCIS WEBSTER
Music by MAURICE JARRE

© 1965, 1966 (Renewed 1993, 1994) Webster Music Co. and EMI Robbins Catalog Inc.
All Rights for Webster Music Co. outside the U.S. and Canada Administered by Almo Music Corp.
All Rights for EMI Robbins Catalog Inc. Administered by EMI Robbins Catalog Inc. (Publishing) and Alfred Music (Print)
International Copyright Secured All Rights Reserved

# SOMEWHERE OUT THERE

from AN AMERICAN TAIL

VIOLIN

Music by BARRY MANN and JAMES HORNER
Lyrics by CYNTHIA WEIL

Copyright © 1986 USI A MUSIC PUBLISHING and USI B MUSIC PUBLISHING
All Rights Controlled and Administered by UNIVERSAL MUSIC CORP. and SONGS OF UNIVERSAL, INC.
All Rights Reserved Used by Permission

# THE SOUND OF MUSIC

from THE SOUND OF MUSIC

VIOLIN

Lyrics by OSCAR HAMMERSTEIN II
Music by RICHARD RODGERS

Copyright © 1959 by Richard Rodgers and Oscar Hammerstein II
Copyright Renewed
Williamson Music, a Division of Rodgers & Hammerstein: an Imagem Company, owner of publication and allied rights throughout the world
International Copyright Secured All Rights Reserved

# SPEAK SOFTLY, LOVE

(Love Theme)

from the Paramount Picture THE GODFATHER

VIOLIN

Words by LARRY KUSIK
Music by NINO ROTA

Copyright © 1972 Sony/ATV Music Publishing LLC
Copyright Renewed
All Rights Administered by Sony/ATV Music Publishing LLC, 424 Church Street, Suite 1200, Nashville, TN 37219
International Copyright Secured All Rights Reserved

# STAR TREK® THE MOTION PICTURE

Theme from the Paramount Picture STAR TREK: THE MOTION PICTURE

VIOLIN

Music by
JERRY GOLDSMITH

**Moderately fast March**

Copyright © 1979 Sony/ATV Music Publishing LLC
All Rights Administered by Sony/ATV Music Publishing LLC, 424 Church Street, Suite 1200, Nashville, TN 37219
International Copyright Secured All Rights Reserved

# SUMMER NIGHTS

from GREASE

VIOLIN

Lyric and Music by WARREN CASEY
and JIM JACOBS

© 1972 WARREN CASEY and JIM JACOBS
© Renewed 2000 JIM JACOBS and THE ESTATE OF WARREN CASEY
All Rights Administered by EDWIN H. MORRIS & COMPANY, A Division of MPL Music Publishing, Inc.
All Rights Reserved

# STAYIN' ALIVE

from the Motion Picture SATURDAY NIGHT FEVER

VIOLIN

Words and Music by BARRY GIBB,
ROBIN GIBB and MAURICE GIBB

Copyright © 1977 by Yvonne Gibb, The Estate Of Robin Gibb, Warner-Tamerlane Publishing Corp. and Crompton Songs LLC
Copyright Renewed
All Rights for Yvonne Gibb and The Estate Of Robin Gibb Administered in the U.S. and Canada by Universal Music - Careers
International Copyright Secured All Rights Reserved

1.
2.

# THE SWEETHEART TREE

from THE GREAT RACE

VIOLIN

Words by JOHNNY MERCER
Music by HENRY MANCINI

**Waltz tempo**

Copyright © 1965 Northridge Music Company, The Johnny Mercer Foundation and Warner-Olive Music LLC
Copyright Renewed
All Rights on behalf of Northridge Music Company Administered by Spirit Two Music
All Rights on behalf of The Johnny Mercer Foundation Administered by WB Music Corp.
All Rights (Excluding Print) for Warner-Olive Music LLC Administered by Universal Music Corp.
Exclusive Worldwide Print Rights for Warner-Olive Music LLC Administered by Alfred Music
All Rights Reserved   Used by Permission

# SWINGING ON A STAR

from GOING MY WAY

VIOLIN

Words by JOHNNY BURKE
Music by JIMMY VAN HEUSEN

Copyright © 1944 by Bourne Co. (ASCAP) and Dorsey Bros. Music, A Division of Music Sales Corporation (ASCAP)
Copyright Renewed
International Copyright Secured All Rights Reserved
Reprinted by Permission

# TAKE MY BREATH AWAY

## (Love Theme)

from the Paramount Picture TOP GUN

VIOLIN

Words and Music by GIORGIO MORODER
and TOM WHITLOCK

Copyright © 1986 Sony/ATV Music Publishing LLC and Budde Music, Inc.
All Rights on behalf of Sony/ATV Music Publishing LLC Administered by Sony/ATV Music Publishing LLC, 424 Church Street, Suite 1200, Nashville, TN 37219
All Rights on behalf of Budde Music, Inc. Administered by WB Music Corp.
International Copyright Secured All Rights Reserved

2.

# TAMMY

from TAMMY AND THE BACHELOR

VIOLIN

Words and Music by JAY LIVINGSTON
and RAY EVANS

Copyright © 1956 JAY LIVINGSTON MUSIC and ST. ANGELO MUSIC
Copyright Renewed
All Rights Reserved Used by Permission

# THANKS FOR THE MEMORY

from the Paramount Picture BIG BROADCAST OF 1938

VIOLIN

Words and Music by LEO ROBIN
and RALPH RAINGER

Copyright © 1937 Sony/ATV Music Publishing LLC
Copyright Renewed
All Rights Administered by Sony/ATV Music Publishing LLC, 424 Church Street, Suite 1200, Nashville, TN 37219
International Copyright Secured All Rights Reserved

# THAT'S AMORÉ
## (That's Love)

from the Paramount Picture THE CADDY

VIOLIN

Words by JACK BROOKS
Music by HARRY WARREN

**Moderately**

Copyright © 1953 Sony/ATV Music Publishing LLC and Four Jays Music
Copyright Renewed
All Rights on behalf of Sony/ATV Music Publishing LLC Administered by Sony/ATV Music Publishing LLC, 424 Church Street, Suite 1200, Nashville, TN 37219
International Copyright Secured All Rights Reserved

# A TIME FOR US

## (Love Theme)

from the Paramount Picture ROMEO AND JULIET

VIOLIN

Words by LARRY KUSIK
and EDDIE SNYDER
Music by NINO ROTA

**Moderately slow**

Copyright © 1968 Sony/ATV Music Publishing LLC
Copyright Renewed
All Rights Administered by Sony/ATV Music Publishing LLC, 424 Church Street, Suite 1200, Nashville, TN 37219
International Copyright Secured All Rights Reserved

# TIME WARP

from THE ROCKY HORROR PICTURE SHOW

VIOLIN

Words and Music by
RICHARD O'BRIEN

Copyright © 1974 (Renewed 2002) Druidcrest Music Ltd.
All Rights Administered by Wixen Music Publishing, Inc.
All Rights Reserved Used by Permission

To Coda
Fine
D.S. al Coda
CODA
D.S.S. al Fine

# TO SIR, WITH LOVE

from TO SIR, WITH LOVE

VIOLIN

Words by DON BLACK
Music by MARC LONDON

**Moderately**

© 1967 (Renewed 1995) SCREEN GEMS-EMI MUSIC INC.
All Rights Reserved International Copyright Secured Used by Permission

# UNCHAINED MELODY

from the Motion Picture UNCHAINED

VIOLIN

Lyric by HY ZARET
Music by ALEX NORTH

© 1955 (Renewed) North Melody Publishing (SESAC) and HZUM Publishing (SESAC) c/o Unchained Melody Publishing, LLC
All Rights Reserved Used by Permission

# TWO HEARTS

from BUSTER

VIOLIN

Words and Music by PHIL COLLINS
and LAMONT DOZIER

Copyright © 1980, 1988 Phil Collins Ltd., Imagem CV and Beau-Di-O-Do Music
All Rights for Phil Collins Ltd. Administered by Imagem CV
All Rights for Beau-Di-O-Do Music Controlled and Administered by Songs Of Universal, Inc.
All Rights Reserved   Used by Permission

1.
2.
3
Fine
D.S. al Fine
(take 2nd ending)

# UP WHERE WE BELONG

from the Paramount Picture AN OFFICER AND A GENTLEMAN

Words by WILL JENNINGS
Music by BUFFY SAINTE-MARIE and JACK NITZSCHE

VIOLIN

Copyright © 1982 Sony/ATV Music Publishing LLC
All Rights Administered by Sony/ATV Music Publishing LLC, 424 Church Street, Suite 1200, Nashville, TN 37219
International Copyright Secured All Rights Reserved

# THE WAY WE WERE

from the Motion Picture THE WAY WE WERE

VIOLIN

Words by ALAN and MARILYN BERGMAN
Music by MARVIN HAMLISCH

© 1973 (Renewed 2001) COLGEMS-EMI MUSIC INC.
All Rights Reserved International Copyright Secured Used by Permission

# WHEN SHE LOVED ME

from Walt Disney Pictures' TOY STORY 2 - A Pixar Film

VIOLIN

Music and Lyrics by
RANDY NEWMAN

© 1999 Walt Disney Music Company and Pixar Talking Pictures
Administered by Walt Disney Music Company
All Rights Reserved. Used by Permission.

# WHEN YOU BELIEVE

(From The Prince of Egypt)

from THE PRINCE OF EGYPT

VIOLIN

Words and Music by
STEPHEN SCHWARTZ

Copyright © 1998 DWA Songs (ASCAP)
All Rights Administered by BMG Rights Management (US) LLC
International Copyright Secured All Rights Reserved

# WHEN YOU WISH UPON A STAR

from Walt Disney's PINOCCHIO

VIOLIN

Words by NED WASHINGTON
Music by LEIGH HARLINE

**Moderately**

Copyright © 1940 by Bourne Co. (ASCAP)
Copyright Renewed
International Copyright Secured All Rights Reserved

# WHERE DO I BEGIN

(Love Theme)

from the Paramount Picture LOVE STORY

VIOLIN

Words by CARL SIGMAN
Music by FRANCIS LAI

Copyright © 1970, 1971 Sony/ATV Music Publishing LLC
Copyright Renewed 1998, 1999 and Assigned to Sony/ATV Music Publishing LLC and Music Sales Corporation
All Rights on behalf of Sony/ATV Music Publishing LLC Administered by Sony/ATV Music Publishing LLC, 424 Church Street, Suite 1200, Nashville, TN 37219
International Copyright Secured All Rights Reserved

# WRITING'S ON THE WALL

from the film SPECTRE

VIOLIN

Words and Music by SAM SMITH
and JAMES NAPIER

Copyright © 2015 Sony/ATV Music Publishing UK Limited, United Lion Music, Naughty Words Limited, Stellar Songs Ltd., U/A Music Inc. and Salli Isaak Songs Ltd.
All Rights on behalf of Sony/ATV Music Publishing UK Limited, United Lion Music, Naughty Words Limited, Stellar Songs Ltd. and U/A Music Inc. Administered by Sony/ATV Music Publishing LLC, 424 Church Street, Suite 1200, Nashville, TN 37219
All Rights on behalf of Salli Isaak Songs Ltd. in the U.S. and Canada Administered by Universal - PolyGram International Tunes, Inc.
International Copyright Secured All Rights Reserved

# YOU LIGHT UP MY LIFE

from YOU LIGHT UP MY LIFE

VIOLIN

Words and Music by
JOSEPH BROOKS

Copyright © 1977 UNIVERSAL - POLYGRAM INTERNATIONAL PUBLISHING, INC. and CURB SONGS
Copyright Renewed
All Rights Reserved Used by Permission

# YOU MUST LOVE ME

from the Cinergi Motion Picture EVITA

VIOLIN

Words by TIM RICE
Music by ANDREW LLOYD WEBBER

**Moderately**

Copyright © 1996 EVITA MUSIC LTD.
All Rights for the U.S. and Canada Controlled and Administered by UNIVERSAL MUSIC CORP.
All Rights Reserved Used by Permission

# 101 SONGS

BIG COLLECTIONS OF FAVORITE SONGS
ARRANGED FOR SOLO INSTRUMENTALISTS.

## 101 BROADWAY SONGS

00154199 Flute..............$15.99
00154200 Clarinet.......$15.99
00154201 Alto Sax........$15.99
00154202 Tenor Sax...$16.99
00154203 Trumpet.......$15.99
00154204 Horn.............$15.99
00154205 Trombone...$15.99
00154206 Violin............$15.99
00154207 Viola..........................................$15.99
00154208 Cello..........................................$15.99

## 101 DISNEY SONGS

00244104 Flute............$17.99
00244106 Clarinet.......$17.99
00244107 Alto Sax.......$17.99
00244108 Tenor Sax...$17.99
00244109 Trumpet.......$17.99
00244112 Horn.............$17.99
00244120 Trombone...$17.99
00244121 Violin............$17.99
00244125 Viola..........................................$17.99
00244126 Cello..........................................$17.99

## 101 MOVIE HITS

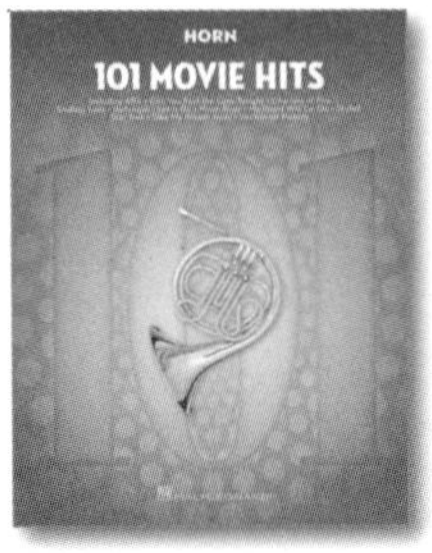


00158087 Flute............$15.99
00158088 Clarinet.......$15.99
00158089 Alto Sax......$15.99
00158090 Tenor Sax...$15.99
00158091 Trumpet........$15.99
00158092 Horn.............$15.99
00158093 Trombone...$15.99
00158094 Violin............$15.99
00158095 Viola..........................................$15.99
00158096 Cello..........................................$15.99

## 101 CHRISTMAS SONGS

00278637 Flute............$15.99
00278638 Clarinet.......$15.99
00278639 Alto Sax......$15.99
00278640 Tenor Sax..$15.99
00278641 Trumpet........$15.99
00278642 Horn............$14.99
00278643 Trombone...$15.99
00278644 Violin............$15.99
00278645 Viola..........................................$15.99
00278646 Cello..........................................$15.99

## 101 HIT SONGS

00194561 Flute..............$17.99
00197182 Clarinet.........$17.99
00197183 Alto Sax........$17.99
00197184 Tenor Sax.....$17.99
00197185 Trumpet.........$17.99
00197186 Horn..............$17.99
00197187 Trombone.....$17.99
00197188 Violin.............$17.99
00197189 Viola..........................................$17.99
00197190 Cello..........................................$17.99

## 101 POPULAR SONGS

00224722 Flute............$17.99
00224723 Clarinet.......$17.99
00224724 Alto Sax......$17.99
00224725 Tenor Sax...$17.99
00224726 Trumpet.......$17.99
00224727 Horn.............$17.99
00224728 Trombone...$17.99
00224729 Violin...........$17.99
00224730 Viola..........................................$17.99
00224731 Cello..........................................$17.99

## 101 CLASSICAL THEMES

00155315 Flute..............$15.99
00155317 Clarinet.........$15.99
00155318 Alto Sax........$15.99
00155319 Tenor Sax.....$15.99
00155320 Trumpet.......$15.99
00155321 Horn..............$15.99
00155322 Trombone....$15.99
00155323 Violin............$15.99
00155324 Viola..........................................$15.99
00155325 Cello..........................................$15.99

## 101 JAZZ SONGS

00146363 Flute.............$15.99
00146364 Clarinet........$15.99
00146366 Alto Sax.......$15.99
00146367 Tenor Sax....$15.99
00146368 Trumpet.......$15.99
00146369 Horn.............$14.99
00146370 Trombone...$15.99
00146371 Violin.............$15.99
00146372 Viola..........................................$15.99
00146373 Cello..........................................$15.99

## 101 MOST BEAUTIFUL SONGS

00291023 Flute.............$16.99
00291041 Clarinet.........$16.99
00291042 Alto Sax........$17.99
00291043 Tenor Sax.....$17.99
00291044 Trumpet.......$16.99
00291045 Horn.............$16.99
00291046 Trombone...$16.99
00291047 Violin............$16.99
00291048 Viola..........................................$16.99
00291049 Cello..........................................$17.99

*See complete song lists and sample pages at www.halleonard.com*

HAL•LEONARD®
www.halleonard.com
*Prices, contents and availability subject to change without notice.*

0423
217

# HAL•LEONARD INSTRUMENTAL PLAY-ALONG

Your favorite songs are arranged just for solo instrumentalists with this outstanding series. Each book includes great full-accompaniment play-along audio so you can sound just like a pro!

Check out **halleonard.com** for songlists and more titles!

### 12 Pop Hits
12 songs
00261790 Flute
00261791 Clarinet
00261792 Alto Sax
00261793 Tenor Sax
00261794 Trumpet
00261795 Horn
00261796 Trombone
00261797 Violin
00261798 Viola
00261799 Cello

### The Very Best of Bach
15 selections
00225371 Flute
00225372 Clarinet
00225373 Alto Sax
00225374 Tenor Sax
00225375 Trumpet
00225376 Horn
00225377 Trombone
00225378 Violin
00225379 Viola
00225380 Cello

### The Beatles
15 songs
00225330 Flute
00225331 Clarinet
00225332 Alto Sax
00225333 Tenor Sax
00225334 Trumpet
00225335 Horn
00225336 Trombone
00225337 Violin
00225338 Viola
00225339 Cello

### Chart Hits
12 songs
00146207 Flute
00146208 Clarinet
00146209 Alto Sax
00146210 Tenor Sax
00146216 Cello
00146212 Horn
00146213 Trombone
00146214 Violin
00146211 Trumpet

### Christmas Songs
12 songs
00146855 Flute
00146858 Clarinet
00146859 Alto Sax
00146860 Tenor Sax
00146862 Trumpet
00146863 Horn
00146864 Trombone
00146866 Violin
00146867 Viola
00146868 Cello

### Contemporary Broadway
15 songs
00298704 Flute
00298705 Clarinet
00298706 Alto Sax
00298707 Tenor Sax
00298708 Trumpet
00298709 Horn
00298710 Trombone
00298711 Violin
00298712 Viola
00298713 Cello

### Disney Movie Hits
12 songs
00841420 Flute
00841687 Oboe
00841421 Clarinet
00841422 Alto Sax
00841686 Tenor Sax
00841423 Trumpet
00841424 Horn
00841425 Trombone
00841426 Violin
00841427 Viola
00841428 Cello

*Prices, contents, and availability subject to change without notice.*

Disney characters and artwork ™ & © 2021 Disney

### Disney Solos
12 songs
00841404 Flute
00841406 Alto Sax
00841407 Horn
00841411 Viola
00841506 Oboe
00841409 Trumpet
00841410 Violin
00841412 Cello
00841405 Clarinet/Tenor Sax
00841408 Trombone/Baritone
00841553 Mallet Percussion

### Dixieland Favorites
15 songs
00268756 Flute
00268757 Clarinet
00268758 Alto Sax
0068759 Trumpet
00268760 Trombone

### Billie Eilish
9 songs
00345648 Flute
00345649 Clarinet
00345650 Alto Sax
00345651 Tenor Sax
00345652 Trumpet
00345653 Horn
00345654 Trombone
00345655 Violin
00345656 Viola
00345657 Cello

### Favorite Movie Themes
13 songs
00841166 Flute
00841167 Clarinet
00841169 Alto Sax
00841168 Trumpet
00841170 Trombone
00841296 Violin

### Gospel Hymns
15 songs
00194648 Flute
00194649 Clarinet
00194650 Alto Sax
00194651 Tenor Sax
00194652 Trumpet
00194654 Trombone
00194655 Violin
00194656 Viola
00194657 Cello

### Great Classical Themes
15 songs
00292727 Flute
00292728 Clarinet
00292729 Alto Sax
00292730 Tenor Sax
00292732 Trumpet
00292733 Horn
00292735 Trombone
00292736 Violin
00292737 Viola
00292738 Cello

### The Greatest Showman
8 songs
00277389 Flute
00277390 Clarinet
00277391 Alto Sax
00277392 Tenor Sax
00277393 Trumpet
00277394 Horn
00277395 Trombone
00277396 Violin
00277397 Viola
00277398 Cello

### Irish Favorites
31 songs
00842489 Flute
00842490 Clarinet
00842491 Alto Sax
00842493 Trumpet
00842494 Horn
00842495 Trombone
00842496 Violin
00842497 Viola
00842498 Cello

### Michael Jackson
11 songs
00119495 Flute
00119496 Clarinet
00119497 Alto Sax
00119498 Tenor Sax
00119499 Trumpet
00119501 Trombone
00119503 Violin
00119502 Accomp.

### Jazz & Blues
14 songs
00841438 Flute
00841439 Clarinet
00841440 Alto Sax
00841442 Tenor Sax
00841441 Trumpet
00841443 Trombone
00841444 Violin

### Jazz Classics
12 songs
00151812 Flute
00151813 Clarinet
00151814 Alto Sax
00151815 Tenor Sax
00151816 Trumpet
00151818 Trombone
00151819 Violin
00151821 Cello

### Les Misérables
13 songs
00842292 Flute
00842293 Clarinet
00842294 Alto Sax
00842295 Tenor Sax
00842296 Trumpet
00842297 Horn
00842298 Trombone
00842299 Violin
00842300 Viola
00842301 Cello

### Metallica
12 songs
02501327 Flute
02501339 Clarinet
02501332 Alto Sax
02501333 Tenor Sax
02501330 Trumpet
02502454 Horn
02501329 Trombone
02501334 Violin
02501335 Viola
02501338 Cello

### Motown Classics
15 songs
00842572 Flute
00842573 Clarinet
00842574 Alto Sax
00842575 Tenor Sax
00842576 Trumpet
00842578 Trombone
00842579 Violin

### Pirates of the Caribbean
16 songs
00842183 Flute
00842184 Clarinet
00842185 Alto Sax
00842186 Tenor Sax
00842187 Trumpet
00842188 Horn
00842189 Trombone
00842190 Violin
00842191 Viola
00842192 Cello

### Queen
17 songs
00285402 Flute
00285403 Clarinet
00285404 Alto Sax
00285405 Tenor Sax
00285406 Trumpet
00285407 Horn
00285408 Trombone
00285409 Violin
00285410 Viola
00285411 Cello

### Simple Songs
14 songs
00249081 Flute
00249093 Oboe
00249082 Clarinet
00249083 Alto Sax
00249084 Tenor Sax
00249086 Trumpet
00249087 Horn
00249089 Trombone
00249090 Violin
00249091 Viola
00249092 Cello
00249094 Mallets

### Superhero Themes
14 songs
00363195 Flute
00363196 Clarinet
00363197 Alto Sax
00363198 Tenor Sax
00363199 Trumpet
00363200 Horn
00363201 Trombone
00363202 Violin
00363203 Viola
00363204 Cello

### Star Wars
16 songs
00350900 Flute
00350913 Oboe
00350903 Clarinet
00350904 Alto Sax
00350905 Tenor Sax
00350906 Trumpet
00350907 Horn
00350908 Trombone
00350909 Violin
00350910 Viola
00350911 Cello
00350914 Mallet

### Taylor Swift
15 songs
00842532 Flute
00842533 Clarinet
00842534 Alto Sax
00842535 Tenor Sax
00842536 Trumpet
00842537 Horn
00842538 Trombone
00842539 Violin
00842540 Viola
00842541 Cello

### Video Game Music
13 songs
00283877 Flute
00283878 Clarinet
00283879 Alto Sax
00283880 Tenor Sax
00283882 Trumpet
00283883 Horn
00283884 Trombone
00283885 Violin
00283886 Viola
00283887 Cello

### Wicked
13 songs
00842236 Flute
00842237 Clarinet
00842238 Alto Sax
00842239 Tenor Sax
00842240 Trumpet
00842241 Horn
00842242 Trombone
00842243 Violin
00842244 Viola
00842245 Cello

HAL•LEONARD®

0122
488

# The Best-Selling Jazz Book of All Time Is Now Legal!

The Real Books are the most popular jazz books of all time. Since the 1970s, musicians have trusted these volumes to get them through every gig, night after night. The problem is that the books were illegally produced and distributed, without any regard to copyright law, or royalties paid to the composers who created these musical masterpieces.

Hal Leonard is very proud to present the first legitimate and legal editions of these books ever produced. You won't even notice the difference, other than all the notorious errors being fixed: the covers and typeface look the same, the song lists are nearly identical, and the price for our edition is even cheaper than the originals!

Every conscientious musician will appreciate that these books are now produced accurately and ethically, benefitting the songwriters that we owe for some of the greatest tunes of all time!

**VOLUME 1**

| | | |
|---|---|---|
| 00240221 | C Edition | $49.99 |
| 00240224 | B♭ Edition | $49.99 |
| 00240225 | E♭ Edition | $49.99 |
| 00240226 | Bass Clef Edition | $49.99 |
| 00286389 | F Edition | $39.99 |
| 00240292 | C Edition 6 x 9 | $39.99 |
| 00240339 | B♭ Edition 6 x 9 | $44.99 |
| 00147792 | Bass Clef Edition 6 x 9 | $39.99 |
| 00200984 | Online Backing Tracks: Selections | $45.00 |
| 00110604 | Book/USB Flash Drive Backing Tracks Pack | $85.00 |
| 00110599 | USB Flash Drive Only | $50.00 |

**VOLUME 2**

| | | |
|---|---|---|
| 00240222 | C Edition | $49.99 |
| 00240227 | B♭ Edition | $49.99 |
| 00240228 | E♭ Edition | $49.99 |
| 00240229 | Bass Clef Edition | $49.99 |
| 00240293 | C Edition 6 x 9 | $39.99 |
| 00125900 | B♭ Edition 6 x 9 | $39.99 |
| 00125900 | The Real Book – Mini Edition | $39.99 |
| 00204126 | Backing Tracks on USB Flash Drive | $55.00 |
| 00204131 | C Edition – USB Flash Drive Pack | $85.00 |

**VOLUME 3**

| | | |
|---|---|---|
| 00240233 | C Edition | $49.99 |
| 00240284 | B♭ Edition | $49.99 |
| 00240285 | E♭ Edition | $49.99 |
| 00240286 | Bass Clef Edition | $49.99 |
| 00240338 | C Edition 6 x 9 | $39.99 |

**VOLUME 4**

| | | |
|---|---|---|
| 00240296 | C Edition | $49.99 |
| 00103348 | B♭ Edition | $49.99 |
| 00103349 | E♭ Edition | $49.99 |
| 00103350 | Bass Clef Edition | $49.99 |

**VOLUME 5**

| | | |
|---|---|---|
| 00240349 | C Edition | $49.99 |
| 00175278 | B♭ Edition | $49.99 |
| 00175279 | E♭ Edition | $49.99 |

**VOLUME 6**

| | | |
|---|---|---|
| 00240534 | C Edition | $49.99 |
| 00223637 | E♭ Edition | $49.99 |

***Also available:***

| | | |
|---|---|---|
| 00154230 | The Real Bebop Book C Edition | $34.99 |
| 00295069 | The Real Bebop Book E♭ Edition | $34.99 |
| 00295068 | The Real Bebop Book B♭ Edition | $34.99 |
| 00240264 | The Real Blues Book | $39.99 |
| 00310910 | The Real Bluegrass Book | $39.99 |
| 00240223 | The Real Broadway Book | $39.99 |
| 00240440 | The Trane Book | $25.00 |
| 00125426 | The Real Country Book | $45.00 |
| 00269721 | The Real Miles Davis Book C Edition | $29.99 |
| 00269723 | The Real Miles Davis Book B♭ Edition | $29.99 |
| 00240355 | The Real Dixieland Book C Edition | $39.99 |
| 00294853 | The Real Dixieland Book E♭ Edition | $39.99 |
| 00122335 | The Real Dixieland Book B♭ Edition | $39.99 |
| 00240235 | The Duke Ellington Real Book | $29.99 |
| 00240268 | The Real Jazz Solos Book | $44.99 |
| 00240348 | The Real Latin Book C Edition | $39.99 |
| 00127107 | The Real Latin Book B♭ Edition | $39.99 |
| 00120809 | The Pat Metheny Real Book C Edition | $34.99 |
| 00252119 | The Pat Metheny Real Book B♭ Edition | $29.99 |
| 00240358 | The Charlie Parker Real Book C Edition | $25.00 |
| 00275997 | The Charlie Parker Real Book E♭ Edition | $25.00 |
| 00118324 | The Real Pop Book C Edition – Vol. 1 | $45.00 |
| 00295066 | The Real Pop Book B♭ Edition – Vol. 1 | $39.99 |
| 00286451 | The Real Pop Book C Edition – Vol. 2 | $45.00 |
| 00240331 | The Bud Powell Real Book | $25.00 |
| 00240437 | The Real R&B Book C Edition | $45.00 |
| 00276590 | The Real R&B Book B♭ Edition | $45.00 |
| 00240313 | The Real Rock Book | $39.99 |
| 00240323 | The Real Rock Book – Vol. 2 | $39.99 |
| 00240359 | The Real Tab Book | $39.99 |
| 00240317 | The Real Worship Book | $35.00 |

**THE REAL CHRISTMAS BOOK**

| | | |
|---|---|---|
| 00240306 | C Edition | $39.99 |
| 00240345 | B♭ Edition | $35.00 |
| 00240346 | E♭ Edition | $35.00 |
| 00240347 | Bass Clef Edition | $35.00 |

**THE REAL VOCAL BOOK**

| | | |
|---|---|---|
| 00240230 | Volume 1 High Voice | $40.00 |
| 00240307 | Volume 1 Low Voice | $40.00 |
| 00240231 | Volume 2 High Voice | $39.99 |
| 00240308 | Volume 2 Low Voice | $39.99 |
| 00240391 | Volume 3 High Voice | $39.99 |
| 00240392 | Volume 3 Low Voice | $39.99 |
| 00118318 | Volume 4 High Voice | $39.99 |
| 00118319 | Volume 4 Low Voice | $39.99 |

**Complete song lists online at www.halleonard.com**

HAL•LEONARD®

0223
318

***Prices, content, and availability subject to change without notice.***